THE MOON

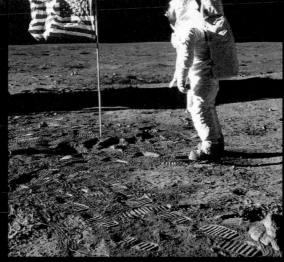

A TRUE BOOK

by
Allison Lassieur

Children's Press®
A Division of Grolier Publishing

New York   London   Hong Kong   Sydney
Danbury, Connecticut

Gemini 3 carried astronauts Virgil Grissom and John Young on three successful orbits around Earth.

Content Consultant
Peter Goodwin
Kent School
Kent, CT

The photograph on the cover shows a close-up image of the full Moon taken through a telescope on Earth. The photograph on the title page shows astronaut Buzz Aldrin saluting an American flag that he and Neil Armstrong placed on the Moon.

Visit Children's Press® on the Internet at:
http://publishing.grolier.com

Library of Congress Cataloging-in-Publication Data

Lassieur, Allison
    The Moon / by Allison Lassieur.
        p. cm. — (A true book)
    Includes bibliographical references and index.
    Summary: Describes the physical characteristics of the Moon and the history of lunar theories, studies, and explorations.
    ISBN: 0-516-22001-2 (lib. bdg.)   0-516-27186-5 (pbk.)
    Moon—Juvenile literature. [1. Moon.] I. Title. II. Series.

QB582 .L37 2000
523.3—dc21   99-055980
                                                                    CIP
                                                                    AC

© 2000 Children's Press®
A Division of Grolier Publishing Co., Inc.
All rights reserved. Published simultaneously in Canada.
Printed in the United States of America.
1 2 3 4 5 6 7 8 9 10 R 09 08 07 06 05 04 03 02 01 00

GROLIER
PUBLISHING

Contents

The face on this Inuit mask represents the spirit of the Moon. The board around the face represents the air, and the feathers represent stars.

What Is the Moon?

In ancient times, people in some countries believed the Moon had special powers. Many cultures worshiped a moon god. The Inuit worshiped a moon god named Igaluk. He also controlled the weather and sea animals. The Greeks believed that Selene was the goddess of the Moon. She drove her silver chariot across the sky every night. Ancient Romans had a moon goddess named Diana.

Since those early times, we have learned a lot about the Moon. In the 1600s, a man named Galileo Galilei used a new invention called a telescope to study the Moon. He realized that the Moon is made of rock. Its surface is covered with tall mountains

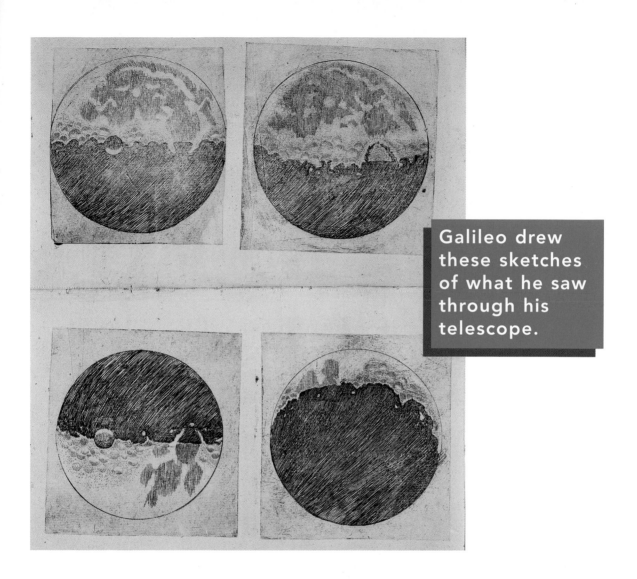

Galileo drew these sketches of what he saw through his telescope.

and giant holes called craters. Galileo drew pictures of what he saw.

Moon on the Move

As time passed, scientists realized that the Moon orbits—or moves in a circle around—our planet. The Moon orbits Earth because our planet pulls on the Moon with a force called gravity. It takes about a month for the Moon to travel around Earth once.

The same side of the Moon always faces Earth. The part of the Moon that we can't see from Earth is called "the far side" of the Moon.

Earth is not the only object that has gravity. All objects in space have some gravity. The bigger an object is, the more gravity it has.

The Sun is the largest object in our solar system so it has the most gravity. That is why Earth and all the other planets orbit

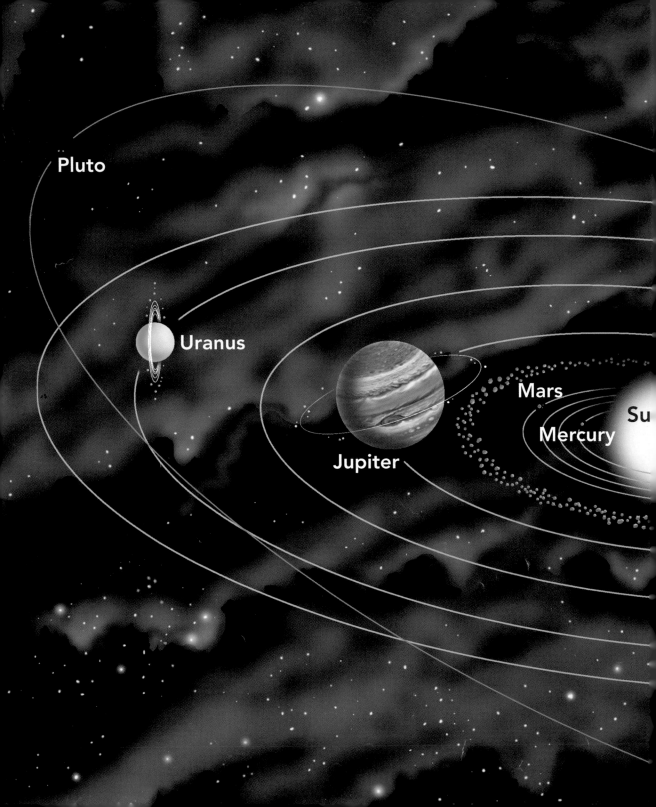

Pluto

Uranus

Jupiter

Mars

Mercury

Su

The Solar System

Venus

Earth

Moon

Saturn

Asteroid Belt

Neptune

As Earth orbits the Sun, the Moon travels around Earth. On Earth, we watch the Sun rise and set every day. Astronauts on the Moon watched Earth rise and set each day.

the Sun. It takes a full year for Earth to orbit the Sun once.

Compared to the Sun, the Moon is a tiny object. It is four times smaller than Earth. The Moon has much less gravity than the Sun, and much less gravity than Earth. But it still has enough gravity to tug on Earth's oceans.

Although the Moon is four times smaller than Earth, the Moon's gravity affects the Earth's oceans.

Like the Moon, Earth spins like a top as it circles the Sun. As Earth spins, the Moon's gravity pulls on the water in the oceans facing it. The water on that side of Earth then bulges toward the Moon. On the opposite side of Earth, another bulge forms to balance the planet. These two bulges follow the Moon as it moves around Earth. They cause high tides. In between the two bulges

The Moon's gravity pulls on Earth and its oceans. At high tide, water washes up onto the beach (left). At low tide, the water washes back out to sea (right).

are low areas called troughs. The troughs create the low tides.

Moon Stories

Almost every culture in the world has beliefs about the Moon. Here are a few of them.

- If you want to be happy, eat a bowl of mashed peas in the moonlight.

- It is lucky to look at the Moon over your right shoulder. Do not look at the Moon over your left shoulder though— that is bad luck!

- If you want warts to disappear, rub them with dirt while looking at the Moon.

The Changing Moon

From Earth, the Moon is the brightest object in the night sky most of the time. Only the Sun is brighter than the Moon. Unlike the Sun, the Moon does not shine on its own. The glow that comes from the Moon is really sunlight bouncing off the Moon's

Only the Sun is brighter than the Moon. Sometimes you can even see the Moon before then Sun sets.

surface. We see different amounts of light reflected on the Moon during different parts of the month.

The Moon looks like it changes shape throughout

the month. Sometimes it looks like a glowing globe. Other times it looks like a sliver of light. These different shapes

Sometimes you can see the entire Moon even though only a tiny sliver is lit up by light from the Sun.

The phases of the moon (from left to right): full moon, half moon, new moon, half moon, and full moon

are called phases. The Moon itself does not change shape. It only seems to change because we see different parts of its sunlit surface as it travels around Earth.

When Earth is between the Sun and the Moon, we see a full moon. This occurs when

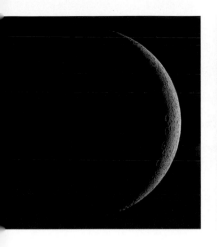

the Sun is shining on the part of the Moon's surface that is facing Earth. Every week, the Moon circles about one-fourth of the way around Earth. After the first week, we can only see light on half of the Moon.

About a week later, the Moon is between the Sun and

Earth. Now the Sun is shining mostly on the side of the Moon that faces away from Earth. That is called a new moon. It looks like the Moon has disappeared completely. The Moon continues to circle the Earth until we see a full moon again. When there are two full moons in one month, the second one is called a blue moon.

The Moon: Hot and Cold

Heat from the Sun warms the Moon. During daytime on the Moon, the temperature reaches a sizzling 230 degrees Fahrenheit (110 degrees Celsius). The hottest temperature ever recorded on Earth was 136°F (58°C).

The Moon's temperature falls to –292°F (–180°C) on the side of the Moon that faces away from the Sun. The coldest temperature ever recorded on Earth was –129°F (–89°C).

Visiting the Moon

For many years, people all over the world dreamed of visiting the Moon. That dream came true for two American astronauts in July 1969. When Neil Armstrong and Buzz Aldrin stepped onto the Moon, their space boots sank into a thick layer of dust.

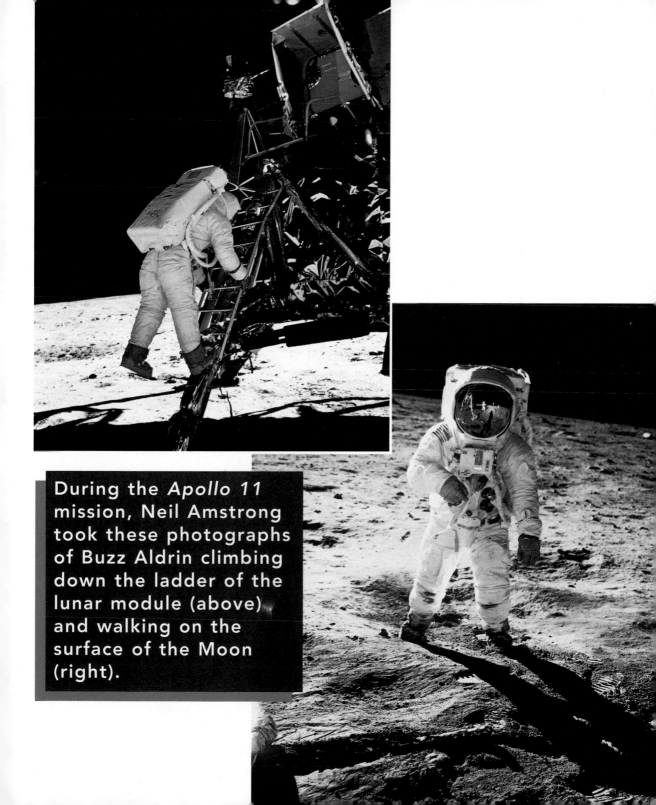

During the *Apollo 11* mission, Neil Amstrong took these photographs of Buzz Aldrin climbing down the ladder of the lunar module (above) and walking on the surface of the Moon (right).

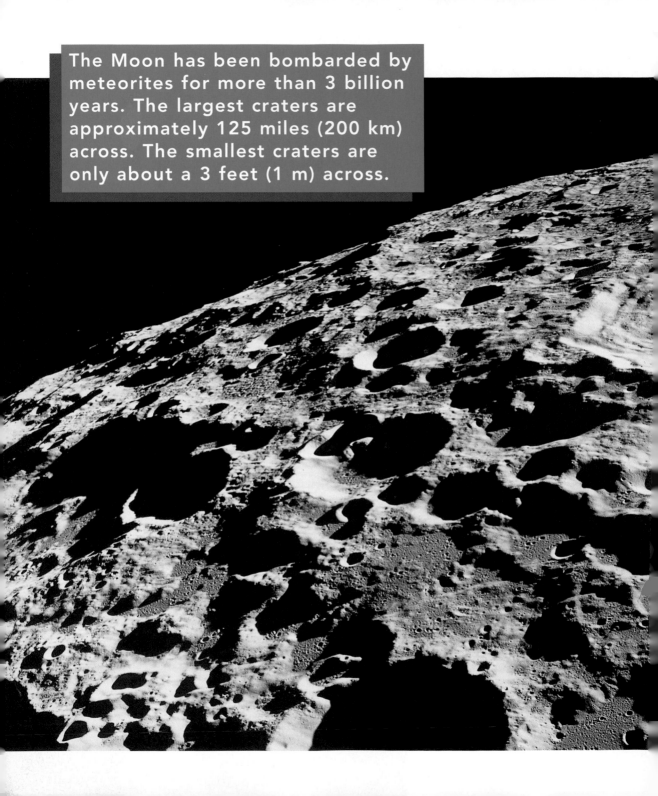

The Moon has been bombarded by meteorites for more than 3 billion years. The largest craters are approximately 125 miles (200 km) across. The smallest craters are only about a 3 feet (1 m) across.

The dust had formed when space rocks called meteorites crashed into the Moon and broke up pieces of the Moon's surface. Some of the rocky meteorites hit the Moon so hard that they made craters. Balls of ice and dust called comets have hit the Moon too.

It took years of hard work to send astronauts to the Moon. In the 1950s, scientists at the National Aeronautics and Space Administration (NASA)

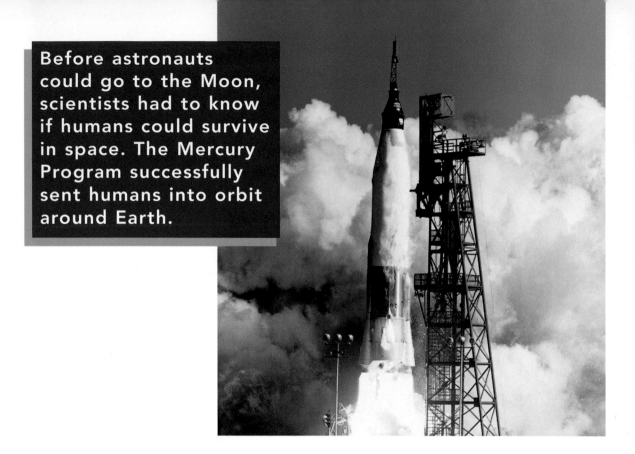

Before astronauts could go to the Moon, scientists had to know if humans could survive in space. The Mercury Program successfully sent humans into orbit around Earth.

began to build rockets and spacecraft that could go into space. During Project Mercury (1961–1963), NASA sent six astronauts into space. Four of them orbited Earth. During

Project Gemini (1965–1966), astronauts spent many days in space. They learned how to walk in space and how to dock with other spacecraft.

During Project Gemini, the first American astronauts left their spacecraft and walked in space.

The *Apollo 11* lunar module landed on the Moon on July 20, 1969.

During Project Apollo (1968–1972), astronauts finally landed on the Moon. The first spacecraft to visit the Moon was *Apollo 11*. Its lunar module landed on an area of the Moon covered with hard lava. This area was called the Sea of Tranquility.

As Neil Armstrong and Buzz Aldrin walked on the Moon's surface, they bounced like kangaroos with every step. Everything weighs less on the

Although the Neil Armstrong and Buzz Aldrin were on the Moon for almost a day, they only spent about 2 hours on the Moon's surface. Neil Armstrong took this picture of Buzz Aldrin.

Moon than on Earth. With their heavy spacesuits on, Armstrong and Aldrin would have weighed 360 pounds (163 kilograms) on Earth. They only weighed 60 pounds (27 kg) on the Moon!

The astronauts spent 21 hours and 37 minutes on the Moon. They spent 2 hours and 31 minutes outside the spacecraft. They collected 50 pounds (23 kg) of soil and rocks, took pictures, and set up some science experiments. Astronaut

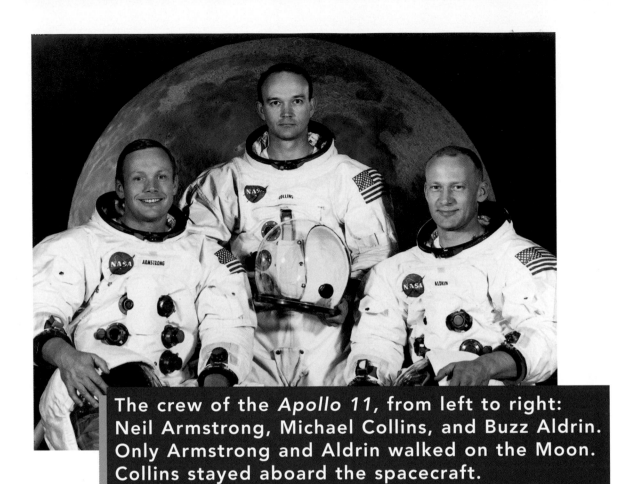

The crew of the *Apollo 11*, from left to right: Neil Armstrong, Michael Collins, and Buzz Aldrin. Only Armstrong and Aldrin walked on the Moon. Collins stayed aboard the spacecraft.

Michael Collins stayed on board the main section of the spacecraft in case there was an emergency.

When the astronauts
returned to Earth, scientists
from all over the world studied
the rock and soil samples.

Scientists studied Moon rocks like this
one to learn more about the Moon.

The lunar roving vehicle was designed especially to travel across the Moon's rocky surface.

They did not find any signs of life, but they learned how old the Moon is and found clues to how it formed.

In the next few years, five more spacecraft landed on the Moon. Some of the astronauts drove across the Moon in a special rover. The last time astronauts visited the Moon was in 1972.

Water and a Moon Base

Even though NASA has not sent any more people to the Moon, scientists have continued to study it. Today, NASA is planning one of the world's largest space projects. They hope to build a Moon base where people can live and work.

In 1998, NASA sent *Lunar Prospector* to the Moon. Scientists programmed the spacecraft to orbit the Moon for a year and then crash into it. The spacecraft's main mission was to look for water on the Moon's surface.

Scientists believe that most of the water on the Moon came from comets that crashed into the Moon.

Some scientists think millions of frozen drops of water might have been brought to the Moon by comets. If there is water on the Moon, it is mixed in with Moon soil and rocks.

The water would have to be dug up, heated, and separated from Moon soil and rocks before humans could drink it. Some scientists say there may be more than 7 billion gallons (26 billion liters)

Some scientists think that there might be enough water on the Moon to support a large group of people living at a moon base.

of water on the Moon. That would be enough to support a city of 4,000 people for 100 years.

If everything works out, construction on the Moon base could start sometime in the twenty-first century. Just think, you or your kids might have a chance to live on the Moon!

To Find Out More

Here are more places to learn about the Moon.

Books

Asimov, Isaac. **The Moon.** Gareth Stevens Publishing, 1994.

Bredeson, Carmen. **The Moon.** Franklin Watts, 1998.

Cole, Michael. **Apollo 11: First Moon Landing.** Enslow Publishers, 1995.

_____. **Moon Base: First Colony in Space.** Enslow Publishers, 1999.

Gardner, Robert. **Science Project Ideas About the Moon.** Enslow Publishers, 1997.

Organizations and Online Sites

The Children's Museum of Indianapolis
3000 N. Meridian Street
Indianapolis, IN 46208-4761
http://www.childrens museum.org/sq1.htm

Check out the SpaceQuest planetarium at the museum and see what shows and exhibits are going on. You can also find other astronomy links at the museum's web site.

Moon Origins, Facts, and Folklore
http://www.arrowweb.com/ M1/themoon/facts.html

Stories, fun facts, and other information about the Moon can be found on this site.

National Aeronautics and Space Administration (NASA)
http://www.nasa.gov

This site has information about every part of space travel, from the Moon missions to life on the Space Shuttle.

National Air and Space Museum Smithsonian Institution
601 Independence Ave., SW
Washington, DC 20560
http://www.nasm.si.edu/

Visit the museum's great website for information about exhibits and special programs.

The Nine Planets
http://www.seds.org/ nineplanets/nineplanets/ nineplanets.html

Jump aboard a spaceship and tour the solar system at this website.

SpaceLink
http://www.spacelink. nasa.gov

This online library has all kinds of space information.

45

Important Words

comet a small ball of ice and rock that orbits the Sun

crater a hole on the surface of an object in space, it is created when a small object crashes into a larger object

gravity a force that pulls objects in space toward one another

high tide when the water on a beach is at its highest point

low tide when water on the beach is at its lowest point

lunar module the section of the Apollo spacecraft that landed on the Moon

meteorite a object that travels through space and crashes into another object

orbit to travel around an object

phase one part of a cycle

telescope an instrument that makes far-away objects look closer

Index

Meet the Author

Allison Lassieur is the author of more than a dozen books for young readers. She enjoys writing about health, history, world cultures, current events, and Native Americans for young readers. She has also written magazines articles for *Disney Adventures, Scholastic News, Highlights for Children,* and *National Geographic World.*

When Ms. Lassieur is not writing, she enjoys reading, playing with her spinning wheel, and participating in historical reenactments.

Photographs ©: Art Resource, NY: 7 (Scala), 4 (Werner Forman Archive/Smithsonian Institution); Corbis-Bettmann: 30; NASA: cover, 1, 2, 12, 25, 26, 28, 29, 32, 34, 35, 36, 42; Photo Researchers: 20, 21 (John Bova), 13 (John Foster), 15 (Andrew J. Martinez), 19 (John Sanford), 18 (Sauzereau); Stocktrek: 39 (Frank Rossotto); Tony Stone Images: 40 (James Balog).